NOT ALL MANGOES ARE SWEET
A book of poetry for deviants

Dear Sara,
I hope you enjoy
my sweet, crass and
poignant words. XO

Marlene Gordon

By
Marlene R Gordon

Cover illustration and book design by Katherine Ross

Printed and bound in Toronto, Canada

ISBN: 978-1-9990139-0-5

Dedicated to my mother, Veronica.
You always inspire me, even if unintentionally.

Contents

Haiku: One Night, Bruised Ego, Swipe for love...or not, Warmth, Kindling, Offline, Mystery, Access Denied, Whores have more fun, Denouement

PART 1

MANGER

Not All Mangoes Are Sweet

On a sunny spring afternoon, I played a soca song for my mother
The singer proclaimed, 'she sweet like a mango!'
My mother swiftly retorted,
'well...not all mangoes are sweet!'
Succinct and profound
Her rebellion has always been quietly subversive
Her genius understated and unacknowledged
The expectation of sweetness
when in fact
you are a bit tart
Better suited for pepper sauce than a saccharine dessert
Maybe I'm a bit of both;
sweet and tart
Nothing wrong with duality
Why must I be one thing?
Later that day, I thanked my mother for her inspiration
She asked what the hell I was talking about
I refreshed her memory
'Not all mangoes are sweet'
To which she replied,
'I said that?'

An Ode to Pork

How supple thy skin of swine?
How protean you are in form
Variable like no other
What say you bacon, prosciutto, mortadella?
How can thy spring from the same mother?

Many abhor thee and think thee vile
But I...
I love thee...
I adore thee...
In all forms you are gracious,
feeding the masses
As they are ignorant and unappreciative of your grace
I see past thy sloth and stink
I view thee as more than cuts of picnic shoulder, tenderloin and hocks
I view thee as sustenance, a gastronomic delight
I shall keep thee at a distance
We shall meet again
in a fortnight

Zesty

I am a bit piquant
Not meant for all palettes
I do come with a warning label
So if you choose to proceed
Do not complain
I burned your tongue
And gave you indigestion

Fruitful

They say you are dead at the root
Unsalvageable
That I should stay away
Before I become just like you
But I do not see death when I look at you

You are salvageable
I will water and prune you
Until you are well again
And then
They will see
That this tree
Will bear many fruit

The Diet

'I'm on the macro diet.' she says
furtively glancing at my fleshy arms.
'It doesn't even feel like I'm restricting myself.
You should try it.
I always eat super clean and organic.
It's really important to me what I put in my body.'

I watch her as she purses her lips,
teeming with hyaluronic acid
I watch her shiny, unnaturally smooth forehead
as she tries to convey emotion
But it remains still;
frozen in time.

'I'm happy the way I am.'
I say with restrained disdain for her...
and her assumption...
that I *should* be unhappy in my skin.
Maybe she sensed my judgement.
Maybe she knew that I knew
that she was deeply uncomfortable in hers.
She countered with a question,
'Is that your real hair?'

So there we sat.
At an impasse.
Judging one another's choices.
You do you, boo!

Cantaloupe

You taste like nothing
And your cousin honeydew
Two basic bitches

Haiku

Coffee Shop

A few furtive glances
Exchanged over iced lattes
Could it be you?...Maybe?

Thirsty

I would lick you from
bow to stern, without hesitation
Let me quench this thirst

PART II

HEAVENLY

BODIES

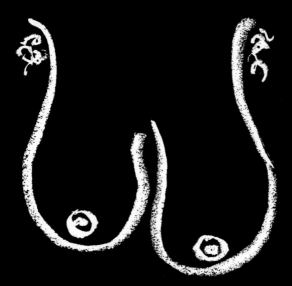

The Red Devil

Every month you announce your arrival
not with a gentle reminder
or a sweet text
you send violent mood swings
preemptive cramps and an insatiable appetite

When you do finally arrive
gently you do not go
you come in the middle of the night
with complete disregard for my serenity
and my high thread count
you stay longer than any polite guest should
and just when I think you've left
I slip on my decent underpants
        ...and there you are
        you ruin everything

What have I done to you?
oh yes...
every month I fail to fulfill my biological duty
and procreate
but you see, I am so much more
no you don't—all you see is an unfulfilled promise

Only a tyrant would tear down my walls
and unleash this crimson carnage
I now understand that I am stuck with you
until I yield
or become barren

A Separate Permission

Your ticket was for vaginal entry only
A special ticket, as it was the first...
You took liberties and also entered through the back
That area was restricted
And required a separate permission and clearance
Way above your pay grade and looks
It's a good thing you had a small penis

Flatulence

You say I fart too much
You tell me I must learn to hold back
Must I suffer in silence to appease you?
I should die a thousand little deaths each day
To appear more ladylike in your eyes?
You cock up your leg
And let 'er rip with aplomb
Then you smile at me
I look at you with reproach
And with the surety and self-importance
That only a man can possess
You say to me
'What? I am a man.'

I quietly collected my things
And as I left I said
'You sir, are the flatulent one!'
I didn't wait for the pungent waft
To hit his nostrils

Beautiful Phallus

Thy rod,
a thing of beauty it is
Always standing at attention
to greet me
Steadfast in its firmness
Glistening and pulsating with life
I shall reward you with my incomparable warmth
A place to call home
A depository for your lacteous eruption

Skin Confetti

The cold, dark winter encroaches
I rush home to find warmth & solace
I hurriedly remove my pants
Dead skin cells pepper the air
Like confetti
       Skin confetti

Me vs. the Camera

You are a fine, rare beauty
Girl, I don't know who told you that, but they lying'
You don't look a day over 30
Remember when you said you would never get filler? You should reconsider
Body looks bangin'
My lie detector determined, that was a lie. Your BMI says you are morbidly obese
I don't need external validation
All those selfies on Instagram tell me otherwise

Nice Lips

Nice lips, he said
He wasn't looking at my face
I don't need labiaplasty

Perenium

In between you are
Fleshy bridge between two worlds
Taint by any other name

I don't know why I'm fat

You don't believe me
When I say I eat healthy
You're right, I don't

Backside

Now it is trendy
To have an inflated rump
Mine is the real deal

Motivation

Exercise now, girl!
Umm maybe later, time is
An arbitrary concept

Toe Licker

You said spread 'em
So I spread my toes apart
Your tongue was vigorous

PART III

LONELY HEARTS

Saudade, Saudade, Saudade

Profound,
utter melancholy
in your absence
is what I feel

A deep longing
for what has passed between us
I know
I know
I know
it may never return
If it does
it certainly won't be the same
I've changed
      so have you

So,
I must hold you in my heart
and in my head
as we were then
Because I may never feel it
that feeling...
In the flesh
again

Entanglement

I try to unfurl myself from you
But the harder I fight
The further entangled I become
Please
Release me

Familiarity

Is it plausible that we've met before?
Not as we are now
 but in other forms
In another time?
On another astral plane?
We are not new to this
you and I
Between us lies an uncanny familiarity
We've been intertwined before
They say history repeats itself
I look forward to our future entanglements

I'll take that one

I sit quietly observing
Wondering when they'll notice me
They don't see my grace
My kindness, my heart
They see her pert breasts and sensuous hair flips
They see the carefree confidence
Of someone who has always be desired
But, when you've always been the 'other'
The filler
The, 'She'll do!'
I know my place is precarious
So I stay quiet,
biding my time
Hoping that one day
Someone with a keen eye
And discerning taste
Will notice me
He'll look past all the bright shiny things
That quickly lose their varnish
He'll admire and study my patina and
know I am to be handled with care
And he'll say
"I'll take that one, she's perfect."

The Sweater

My search was long and arduous
I tried on many things...too many things
I couldn't understand why they did not fit
They were too itchy, too hot, too tight, too bulky
Was I malformed? Was I unfit?
Maybe I didn't deserve a sweater
Maybe I didn't deserve warmth and comfort
Perhaps I was meant to live this life in a sheer cotton t-shirt
That would pill and gather holes

But then...
I realized the problem was
I'd been trying on acrylic and poly-blend
When what I wanted was
Alpaca, merino and cashmere
It was in that moment, when I became clear
You made yourself known
I put you on and immediately knew
There would never be a need for any other sweater
You would provide all the warmth and comfort I needed
I would hand wash you with fine linen wash
And lay you flat to dry
For you are far too precious
To shrink in the dryer

Waiting

Yesterday, I cried a deep, guttural cry
because you have yet to appear
I cried with profound intensity and sadness
because I started to believe you didn't exist
yesterday, I cried
because I decided to permanently close
the vacancy I had left for you in my heart
it had been empty for far too long

I am a cynic
I do not believe until I am shown
no one has shown me
only left mars and dents
so show me
where are you?
yesterday, I ran out of tears

Today, I awake anew
my heart, bursting at the seams
with the knowledge that even though it is full
there will always be space for you
today, I wake with a smile upon my face
because I *know* you exist
I feel you in everything I do
today, I awoke with brighter vision
so I could clearly and precisely see you
when you decide to make yourself known

Infinite

You'd like me to quantify what it is I feel for you
I'm afraid you have given me an impossible task
One cannot quantify the unquantifiable
There is no numeric value I can assign
There are no words gracious or eloquent enough
To adequately describe the breadth and depth
For which I feel for you

So let me just say this...
My love for you is
Boundless
Impenetrable
&
Infinite

Bruised Ego

I think I like you
You're not interested...
Terrible taste, Sir

Swipe for love...or not

Swipe left or swipe right
Find love, find a dalliance
Find disappointment

Offline

Where have you gone?
How will I keep tabs on you?
'You could just call me.'

Haiku

Access Denied

Your access to me
Was on a trial basis
You are not worthy

Haiku

Whores have more fun

Chastity is boring
You should have sucked that dick
More stories to tell

PART IV

REVELATIONS

A Trifle Gaudy

I've been told I am:
– a trifle gaudy
– a skosh garish
– a smidgen ostentatious
But my friend,
perfection sometimes lies
just skirting the line
between sacrilege
and the sublime

The Internal Process

I should share this with the world.

~~They won't like it. It's trash.~~

But it's bold. Maybe even revolutionary.

~~No it ain't. It's been done before.~~

What if they don't get it?

~~They won't. It's esoteric and contrived.~~

My friends like it.

~~Well your friends are twats, enabling your stupidity.~~

Well, I'm going to share it anyway.

~~You'll make a mockery of yourself.~~

You're right. Just forget it...

~~That's better. I knew you didn't have it in you.~~

Why do you always do this to me?

~~I'm just trying to spare you the embarrassment when things dont work out~~

Taking a risk is better than stagnation. If I fail, I fail. But what if I fly?

~~You won't fly. You'll crash and burn.~~

We'll see.

🔇✕

Anomaly

You are an anomaly
A deviation in the code
You are not meant to be like the others
This is where you find the most discomfort
When you try to assimilate
Assimilation = dearth of creativity
Assimilation = acceptance of banality
The greatest tragedy in life
Is donning a costume of befitting humanity
Shed the artifice and wear yourself

Am I your Queen or nah?

You like full lips
and a round, fat ass
but you don't like it on my brown skin
why not?
it's just like yours
you prefer it on a much less pigmented canvas
on a body for which it is not innate
but purchased

You say I am too greedy
when I ask for things
that I see you give freely to other women
if I challenge you
I am combative
when she does, she is spicy
you place me on the back of a dusty shelf
and her on a pedestal
I support you
I won't let others denigrate you
but you
          you throw me to the wolves
and join them
as they tear my flesh apart

Know Thyself

'Who are you?' they ask.
As if I have an honest answer I'm willing to share.
As if I'm bold enough to tell them the truth.
Who shall I play?
What answer will be most palatable?
They ask me this question
because they want a self-deprecating, modest reply.
'We are different things to different people,' I say.
Some will tell you I'm kind and patient.
Some will say I'm curt and abrasive.
To some I have wealth of knowledge, to others I am a forlorn simpleton.
Who I am to you is a reflection of yourself.
Who I am to myself is entirely different.

So let's reframe the question.
Who am I at my core?
Private.

Wake up

Nothing has changed
There is such comfort in sameness
But there is also stagnation
You seem to expect a different outcome
When you keep doing the same shit
That by definition is

    INSANITY

Listen

I assure you
my feelings are not without merit
it is visceral
I know it in my core
I am right
but you must learn it
on your own
because my words you do not heed

Lessons

I do not recall sending for you
and yet here you are
enthralled by and entangled in my affairs
—uninvited guest
I will not welcome you with pleasantries
I will not pour you a drink
or treat you with an ounce of civility
I will do for you
what I do for all of those who come for me
when I did not send for them
A verbal evisceration
A lesson in reverence and minding your own damn business
And a reminder not to come for me
Unless explicitly I send for you

Conversing With the Full Moon

Like you, I want to be fully illuminated
Tell me, what's it like to feel whole?
To shine bright without the darkness impeding

I bet you have stories to tell
Strange occurrences
Changing tides
Tell me your secrets

Tonight you are whole
But the rest of the time you're just like me
Waxing and waning
Between darkness and light

M

Why did you have to leave so soon?
It was before your time
I'm sure of that
I wish you would have shown yourself
The same grace that you extended to others
Perhaps the small, frequent mars
Left a big gaping chasm
You thought irreparable
Maybe all of us could have helped you heal
Maybe that's wishful thinking
I hope the pain that gripped you in life
Slipped away
As you did
Into the great beyond

Spinster

You are a woman of a certain age
You shouldn't be so selective
Your time is running out
Your reservoir depleting
Fine lines form around your eyes
Your youthful fervour and exuberance have dissipated
Replaced by pragmatism and a healthy disdain for tomfoolery

The longer you sit on the shelf
The lower your value
The less they'll notice you
You'll be on clearance soon...
Spruce it up!
Turn down your volume!
Soften your edges!
Serve it up on a platter!
Remember, you are only for consumption
So you must be digestible

If you end up alone
You only have yourself to blame
Perhaps you didn't try hard enough
To make yourself palatable

Spinster Nouveau

Funny, there is no word for a woman of a certain age
Who is happily untethered
A woman who is selective
Because she has carefully curated her life
She considers her space sacred
Reserved for the deserved
She knows her eggs are depleting
Because she is oft reminded of it
She has lived and learned and has no time for foolishness

She is ok with sitting on the shelf
Because she's not a perishable item
She is uncorked only for those who can appreciate her depth
She will not turn down her volume   and
                                                      richness
She was silenced for too long
Now that she's found her voice, you cannot quiet her
Her edges are sharp only to those who would do her harm
She is not here for your consumption
If you cannot digest her
Perhaps your palate isn't refined enough

You Ain't Like All Those Other Heauxs

Never trust a man
that extols your virtue and sanity
over all other women
because before you know it
—you will be all other women
he will tell tales of you
and your irrational behaviour
whilst painting himself the protagonist
negating all his ills and atrocities

So, when you hear a man proclaim
that all his ex-lovers are crazy
he either has a proclivity for insanity
or he is the cause of it

Unanimous

We took a vote
It was unanimous
We've decided
You are spectacular
Perhaps you'll join us
In believing that

Words Have Weight

It is true
Words do have weight
I feel them as I tuck them under my tongue
Holding them back so you may speak freely
Sometimes I swallow them for you
But they are growing anxious
My words want their turn
They become sharper and more pungent
The longer they brew

When they escape
You say the weight of them
Is too much for you
They are far too heavy / too wicked / too jagged
You say they are unlike me
But they are indeed a part of me
If you'd let me speak sooner
They would have been much sweeter
And as light as a feather

Strange-ling

Bask in your strangeness
The others won't understand
It's not for them to

Cantankerous

Earned with old age
Too many wrinkles to care
Give up your seat, now

Pleasantries

What's new with you?
I have genital warts
How are you doing?

Mercy

Showing grace to those
That don't deserve your kindness
Even if begrudgingly

Deference

Take heed of those that
paved the way in the face
of cruelty and hate

Haiku

Passive Aggressive

Read my energy
You should know how I feel
Why don't you get it?

Positive Thinking

Today will be great
Everything will go your way!
Just kidding, it won't

Concealed Poverty

Let's get a latte!
I have $34 in my account
Everything is fine

DIM

when all seems lost
when life seems grim
when your heart is in tatters
when your inner light has gone dim
when you don't remember
what is love and what is bliss
please do remember
this
and
only this

time here is finite
and so is pain
and happiness, though fleeting
will return to you again
the clouds will part
and oh the sun will shine
kissing your shoulders
as you lay in the grass supine

when you are found
when life is bliss
when your heart is full
and you've been kissed
please share your light
from deep within
for those in need
for those still dim